*The
Little Love
Book*

अग्निमदन

agnimadana
the maddening fire of sexual love

अदेह

adeha
bodiless, divine love

anaga
bodiless, god of love

अनुरक्ति
anurakti
devoted affection

अनुराग
anurāga
attachment

अनुरागवत्
anurāgavat
in love with

अनुरति

anurati
love, affection, attachment

अनुरुध्

anurudh
to surround or confine with love

अपत्यस्नेह

apatyasneha
love for one's own children

अपह्नव

apahnava
appeasing and concealing love

अपाङ्ग

apāṅga
bodiless love

अभिहर्यति

abhiharyati
to love, to call near

अवसन्न

avasanna
exhausted from doubtful or unsuccessful love

अवस्कन्न

avaskanna
attacked by love

अस्पन्द

aspanda
unquivering or unmoving in love

आका

ākā
to endeavor, to obtain, to love

आसक्तभाव

āsaktabhāva
having one's affection fixed on

इच्छापित

icchāpita
caused to love

ई

ī
consciousness and perception of compassion or
consideration,
god of love

उज्ज्वल

ujjvala
luminous blazing up of beauty, full blown,
expanded love and passion

utkaṇṭhita
longing for and regretting love

उत्कथ्

utkvath
to be consumed by love

उन्मदन

unmadana
inflamed with love

कटाक्षविशिख

kaṭākṣaviśikha
an arrow-like look of love

कन्दर्प

kandarpa
a great wantonness or inflamer

कन्दर्पकूप

kandarpakūpa
the well of love

कर्व

karva
love, a mouse or rat

कान्ति

kānti
beauty enhanced by love

काम

kāma
erotic, sensual love, god of love

कामदमिनी

kāmadaminī
she who tames love,
a passionate woman

कामदेव

kāmadeva
the god of love that creates, preserves or destroys at will

कामबद्ध

kāmabaddha
bound by love

काममूत

kāmamūta
strongly impelled by love

कामरस

kāmarasa
enjoyment of sexual love

कामवल्लभ

kāmavallabha
love's favorite

कामाग्नि

kāmāgni
fire of love

कामाग्निसंदीपन

kāmāgnisaṃdīpana
kindling the fire of lust or sexual love

कामातुर

kāmātura
love sick

कामाधिष्ठित

kāmādhiṣṭhita
influenced or dominated by love

कामान्ध

kāmāndha
blinded by passion or lust

कामार्थिन्

kāmārthin
amorous

कामासक्ति

kāmāsakti
addiction to love

कामोन्मत्त

kāmonmatta
mad with love

कामिता

kāmitā
the state of a lover, desire

कामिन्

kāmin
longing after, anxious husband

कृष्णप्रेमामृत

kṛṣṇapremāmṛta
nectar of love of Krishna, associated with the word *ambrosia*

कैशिकी

kaiśikī
graceful style in the passion of love

खरीवात्सल्य

kharīvātsalya
maternal love of a she-mule

गदयित्नु
gadayitnu
libidinous, lustful

गन्धर्वविवाह
gandharvavivāha
a marriage proceeding entirely from love without
ceremonies and without consulting relatives

गोपीप्रेमामृत
gopīpremāmṛta
nectar of (Krishna's) love for the cowherdesses

चन्द्रसचिव

candrasaciva
who has the moon for a friend,
god of love

चित्तज

cittaja
heart-born

चित्तप्रमाथिन्

cittapramāthin
confusing the mind, exciting one's passion or love

जन्मवात्सल्य

janmavātsalya
love for one's native country

जातकाम

jātakāma
fallen in love

जुष्टि

juṣṭi
love, service

तारामैत्रक

tārāmaitraka
star friendship, spontaneous love

दशकामजव्यसन

daśakāmajavyasana
10 vices arising from love of pleasure: hunting, gambling, sleeping by day, censoriousness, excess with women, drunkenness, an inordinate love for dancing, singing, and music, and useless travel

ध्वस्तप्रेमन्

dhvastapreman
feeling of vanished love

नर्मस्फोट

narmasphoṭa
first symptoms of love

नायिका

nāyikā
woman wise in love and life's pleasures,
embodying Shakti (energy) without which even
Lord Shiva would not be able to open his eyes

##

naiḥsnehya
absence of love

परोक्षमन्मथ

parokṣamanmatha
inexperienced in love

पुत्रस्नेहमय

putrasnehamaya
full of love for a son

पुष्प

puṣpa
blossoming, the menstrual flux, declaration of love

पूर्वराग

pūrvarāga
earliest affection, love which springs from some
previous cause

प्रगम

pragama
first manifestation of love,
first advance of courtship

प्रणी

praṇī
to manifest love, affection, desire

प्रणयकुपित

praṇayakupita
angry through love, feigning anger

प्रणयमान

praṇayamāna
love-pride, jealousy

प्रणयवचन

praṇayavacana
a declaration of love

प्रणयविमुख

praṇayavimukha
averse from love

प्रणयस्पृश्

praṇayaspṛś
romantic touch which excites love

प्रणयोन्मुख

praṇayonmukha
expectant through love

प्रतिनृत्

pratinṛt
to dance before (in token of love)

प्रतिहर्यति

pratiharyati
to accept love gladly

प्रपूरण

prapūraṇa
filling up and increasing love

प्ररोचन

prarocana
seducing into love (as a spell)

प्रस्नुतस्तनी

prasnutastanī
excess of maternal love,
having breasts that flow with milk

प्राणान्तिक

prāṇāntika
life endangering, desperate love

प्रिय

priya
beloved, favorite

प्रियजीवितता

priyajīvitatā
love of life

प्रियता

priyatā
being fond of, dear to

प्रीति

prīti
joy or gratification personified, pleasure, affection, love

प्रीतिकर

prītikara
inspiring love, causing pleasure

प्रीतिकर्मन्

prītikarman
act of love or friendship

प्रीतिद

prītida
giving pleasure which inspires love,
a jester or buffoon in a play

प्रीतिदाय

prītidāya
gift of love, a present made with love

प्रीतिधन

prītidhana
money given from love

प्रीतिमत्

prītimat
pleasing or gratifying with love

प्रीतिवर्धन

prītivardhana
increasing love or joy

प्रीतिस्निग्ध

prītisnigdha
eyes which are moist through love

प्रेमबन्ध

premabandha
the ties of love

प्रेमर्द्धि

premarddhi
ardent love, increase of love

प्रेमलतिका

premalatikā
the vine of love

प्रेमवत्

premavat
full of love

प्रेमविश्वासभूमि

premaviśvāsabhūmi
object of love and confidence

प्रेमसागर

premasāgara
an ocean of love

प्रेमाकर

premākara
abundance of love

प्रेमार्द्र

premārdra
overflowing with love

प्रेमणीय

premaṇīya
fit for exciting love

प्रेम्णा

premṇā
through love

प्रौढ

prauḍha
a bold, unafraid woman who stands in no awe of
her partner, mature in love

बन्धुप्रीति

bandhuprīti
love of friends

ब्राह्मणकाम्या

brāhmaṇakāmyā
love for Brahman
(cosmic principle or divine power)

भक्ति

bhakti
love of god, devotion to god

भग

bhaga
sexual passion, a vagina or man's perineum, good fortune

भर्तृस्नेह

bhartṛsneha
love of a husband

भर्तृस्नेहपरीत

bhartṛsnehaparīta
filled with love for a husband

भवभाव

bhavabhāva
love of worldly existence

भवत्स्नेह

bhavatsneha
the love for your ladyship or for you

भाव

bhāva
love, emotion or state

भावज

bhāvaja
love born of the heart

भावबन्धन

bhāvabandhana
joining hearts

भावाकूत

bhāvākūta
the first emotions of love

भावैकरस

bhāvaikarasa
influenced solely by love

मदकलयुवति
madakalayuvati
a young woman intoxicated with love

मदालापिन्
madālāpin
uttering sounds of love

मदनकण्टक
madanakaṇṭaka
erection of hair caused by the thrill of love

मदनक्लिष्ट

madanakliṣṭa
sweet post-coital exhaustion, suffering lovers' games

मदनगोपाल

madanagopāla
herdsman of love

मदनबाधा

madanabādhā
lovesick, the pain of love

मदनभवन

madanabhavana
abode of love or matrimony

मदनमय

madanamaya
entirely under the influence of the god of love

मदनवह्निशिखावली

madanavahniśikhāvalī
the flame of the fire of love

मदनशिखिपीडा

madanaśikhipīḍā
the pain caused by the fire of love

मदनसंदेश

madanasaṃdeśa
a message of love

मदनार्णव

madanārṇava
sea of love

मदनोत्सुक
madanotsuka
pining or languid with love

मदनोदय
madanodaya
raising of love

मदनीय
madanīya
intoxicating, exciting passion

मनःसङ्ग

manaḥsaṅga
fixing the thoughts on the beloved, attachment of the mind

मनसिज

manasija
heart-born

मनसिजतरु

manasijataru
love conceived as a tree, a tree that grows and blossoms through the water of love, nourishment through love

मनसिमन्द

manasimanda
slow or inert in love

मनसिमन्दरुज्

manasimandaruj
pain of love

मनोज

manoja
mind-born love

मनोभव

manobhava
arising in the mind, love

मनोभवद्रुम

manobhavadruma
love compared to a tree, tree of love

मन्मथ

manmatha
amorous passion, god of love

मन्मथबन्धु

manmathabandhu
friend of love, the moon

मन्मथयुद्ध

manmathayuddha
strife of love, an amorous contest

मन्मथसमान

manmathasamāna
feeling similar love

मन्मथानन्द

manmathānanda
love's joy, a type of mango

मन्मथानल

manmathānala
fire of love

मन्मथाविष्ट

manmathāviṣṭa
penetrated by love

मन्मथोद्दीपन

manmathoddīpana
the act of kindling or inflaming love

मान्मथ

mānmatha
produced by love, filled with love

महानुराग

mahānurāga
great love, excessive affection

मुषितत्रप

muṣitatrapa
one whose sense of shame has been stolen by love

मोहनास्त्र

mohanāstra
a weapon which fascinates the one against whom
it is directed, weapon of the god of love

मोहित

mohita
infatuated or deluded by love

यौवनोद्भेद

yauvanodbheda
the ardor of youthful passion,
god of love

रङ्ग

raṅga
a dancing place, a field of battle, love

रञ्जक

rañjaka
a painter, one who dyes, an inciter of affection,
cinnabar

रणरणक

raṇaraṇaka
anxious regret for some beloved object

रत

rata
beloved, sex

रति

rati
amorous enjoyment

रतिज्ञ

ratijña
skilled in the art of love

रतिरणधीर

ratiraṇadhīra
bold and energetic in love's contests

रतिरस

ratirasa
as sweet as love

रतिसंहित

ratisaṃhita
accompanied with love, abounding with affection

रतिसर्वस्व

ratisarvasva
the whole essence of love

रमति

ramati
liking to remain in one place, a lover, paradise, heaven, god of love

रस

rasa
the sap or juice of plants or fruit, semen, a taste for
love, the essence of an emotion

रसवत्

rasavat
full of sap, juicy, succulent, possessing love

रसाभ्यन्तर

rasābhyantara
filled with water or love

रहःस्थ

rahaḥstha
standing in secrecy, being in the enjoyment of love

राग

rāga
inflammation, vehement desire, loveliness,
beauty, an order of sound

रागच्छन्न

rāgacchanna
love covered, god of love

रूढप्रणय

rūḍhapraṇaya
one whose love has grown strong

रूढरागप्रवाल

rūḍharāgapravāla
the tree of love in which the sprouts of affection
have grown strong

रूपास्त्र

rūpāstra
having beauty for a weapon,
god of love

रोचन

rocana
bright, shining, radiant, an arrow of the god of love

लालित

lālita
caressed or fondled, pleasure, love

ललिता

lalitā
a wanton woman

लास्य
lāsya
a dance representing the emotions of love

लोककाम्या
lokakāmyā
a woman who desires to love many

लोकानुराग
lokānurāga
desiring many lovers

लुब्ध

lubha
to love, desire greatly, eager longing for, to
become perplexed, crazy or disturbed, thought to
be the origin of *love* in English

वनच्छन्दता

vanacchandatā
longing for the forest

वल्लभता

vallabhatā
the state of being beloved

वासयति

vāsayati
to bestow by shining upon, to love,
to make love to

वात्सल्य

vātsalya
affection or tenderness towards
one's children

वामशील

vāmaśīla
timid in love, coy

वाल्लभ्य

vāllabhya
being beloved or favorite,
love, tenderness

विकारिन्

vikārin
undergoing change, falling in love

विगतस्नेह

vigatasneha
void of affection, lost love

विगतस्नेहसौहृद
vigatasnehasauhṛda
one who has relinquished love and friendship

विधूनन
vidhūnana
agitation in love, repulsion

विभाविन्
vibhāvin
arousing emotion, mighty, powerful

विषण्णता

viṣaṇṇatā
dejection, sadness, lassitude, unsuccessful love

विषयिन्

viṣayin
attachment to worldly or
carnal objects, the ego

विस्मापन

vismāpana
an illusionist, god of love,
love which astonishes

विहृत

vihṛta
hesitation, reluctance, bashful silence of female love

व्रणितहृदय

vranitahrdaya
heart-stricken

व्यसन

vyasana
evil passion which arises from love of pleasure or anger, fruitless effort, addiction to

शामान्तक

śamāntaka
destroyer of tranquility, god of love, broken love,
tranquility destroyed by love

स्मर्तव्यात्मा

smartavyatma
whose body is only a memory,
god of love

शश्वत्काम

śaśvatkāma
always intent on love

शिखा

śikhā
fever of love, a point, a nipple, a pointed flame,
a ray of light,
a branch which takes root

शुचि

śuci
sexual love, radiant, white, pure, fire

शृङ्

śṛṅga
excess of love, the rising of passion, the horn of an
animal

श्रृङ्गार

śṛṅgāra
the erotic sentiment

श्रृङ्गारगर्व

śṛṅgāragarva
the pride of love

श्रृङ्गारचेष्टित

śṛṅgāraceṣṭita
a gesture of love

श्रृङ्गारजन्मन्
śṛṅgārajanman
born from desire

श्रृङ्गारलज्जा
śṛṅgāralajjā
shame or modesty caused by love

श्रृङ्गारशूर
śṛṅgāraśūra
a hero of love

श्रृङ्गारैकरस

śṛṅgāraikarasa
one whose sole feeling is love

श्रृङ्गारण

śṛṅgāraṇa
feigning love

श्रृङ्गारिन्

śṛṅgārin
feeling love, red stained

शृङ्गारीय

śṛṅgārīya
to long for love

शौर्यौदर्यशृङ्गारमय

śauryaudaryaśṛṅgāramaya
composed of love, heroism and generosity

संस्तवप्रीति

saṃstavaprīti
love proceeding from acquaintance

सकाम

sakāma
full of love, satisfying desires,
acting with free will

सखीस्नेह

sakhīsneha
love for female friends

सत्यता

satyatā
love of truth

सम्प्रीति

samprīti
complete satisfaction, love for

सम्भोग

sambhoga
carnal love, successful love, complete enjoyment, pleasure, delight in

सम्भृतस्नेह

sambhṛtasneha
full of love for

सम्मति

sammati
love, harmony, agreement

सम्मोहित

sammohita
stupefied, bewildered, enraptured, fascinated

सरस

sarasa
full of love, a lake or pond, juicy, fresh

सलज्जितस्नेहकरुणम्

salajjitasnehakaruṇam
with love, bashfulness and compassion

सश‍ृङ्गारकम्

saśṛṅgārakam
with passionate, tender love

सुभक्ति

subhakti
love out of great devotion

सुभगता
subhagatā
conjugal felicity, love

सुशीमकाम
suśīmakāma
deeply in love

सेवितमन्मथ
sevitamanmatha
addicted to love or amorous enjoyments

स्थिरानुराग

sthirānurāga
constant in love and affection

स्नेह

sneha
love and friendship, tenderness, oiliness,
glossiness

स्नेहकर्तृ

snehakartṛ
showing affection or love

स्नेहगुरु

snehaguru
heavy hearted from love

स्नेहप्रसर

snehaprasara
gush of love

स्नेहबद्ध

snehabaddha
bound by love

स्नेहबन्ध

snehabandha
the bonds of love

स्नेहभूमि

snehabhūmi
one worthy of love, an object of affection,
a substance yielding oil or grease

स्नेहसंज्वरवत्

snehasaṃjvaravat
smitten with the fever of love

स्नेहाकुल
snehākula
agitated by love

स्मर
smara
love recollection

स्मरकूपिका
smarakūpaka
well of love, the vagina

स्मरगुरु

smaraguru
love teacher

स्मरज्वर

smarajvara
love fever, ardent love

स्मरदशा

smaradaśā
ten states of the body produced by love: joy of the eyes, pensive reflection, desire, sleeplessness, emaciation, indifference to external objects, abandonment of shame, infatuation, fainting away, death

स्मरदुर्मद

smaradurmada
intoxicated by love

स्मरनिपुण

smaranipuṇa
skilled in the art of love

स्मरपीडित

smarapīḍita
tormented by love

स्मरभासित

smarabhāsita
inflamed by love

स्मरभू

smarabhū
arisen from love

स्मरमय

smaramaya
produced by love

स्मराकुलित

smararuj
attacked by god of love, symptoms of love sickness, affected by love

स्मरवल्लभ

smaravallabha
love's favorite

स्मरवृद्धि

smaravṛddhi
love's increase, a plant whose seed is an aphrodisiac

स्मराकृष्ट

smarākṛṣṭa
overcome by love

स्मरातुर

smarātura
eager for lovemaking, lust

स्मरान्ध

smarāndha
blind with lust or love

स्मृतिजात

smṛtijāta
memory born love

स्वानुभाव

svānubhāva
love for property

स्वान्तज

svāntaja
heart born love

हर्तु

hartu
great love, the seizer

हार्द

hārda
being in the heart

हृच्छय

hṛcchaya
the protective shadow of the heart, feeling the relief of love from the harshness of the world.

हृच्छयपीडित

hṛcchayapīḍita
tormented by love

हृच्छयाविष्टचेतन

hṛcchayāviṣṭacetana
having a heart penetrated by love

हेवाकस

hevākasa
whimsical, capricious love

Dear friend,
Dear you,
Dear me,

Remember:
Contraction never stops asking for expansion.
Anger never stops asking for forgiveness.
Suffering never stops asking for pleasure.
Fear never stops asking for love.

Go to love.

Ask your body. It does not lie.

Los Angeles, California
September 2017

Notes on Sanskrit:

Sanskrit can be seen as a system of codifying poetry. Infinite words and their use are possible when combined within the context of creativity. It is a language of sound with a focus on the expression of essence - the intrinsic quality of a state or idea. It is believed that each sound and letter in Sanskrit contains a transmission of energy when spoken aloud or read silently. Here, language can be seen as a bridge between the creative and the created.

© *2017 Elyse Poppers*
All Rights Reserved